D1498930

THE PARADOX

*A conversation
of life*

Eugene Charles

Alexandria Publishing
163 3rd Ave. #139
New York, NY 10003

Printed in the United States of America
0987654321

Library of Congress Catalog Card Number 94-96695
ISBN 0-9644217-0-4

For information, write or call Alexandria Publishing
The Paradox Division 1-800-351-5450

Prelude

Humans, as a whole, have a tendency to be misguided. We struggle against the waves for objects of little or no importance instead of loosely riding the waters to reach the riches abundantly scattered at our shores.

Not until we lose time, love or health does our attention become calibrated to that which truly deserves the priority of our thoughts, words and actions.

How do you know where to direct your energies? How do you change destruction into construction? If you have wasted time, life, and spirit, and think you have missed the sweetness of opportunity, who can recapture all these energies for you?

Do not look outside of yourself. Observe the demise of those who rely solely on others for guidance, thinking that someone other than themself would know what is best for them. Perhaps it is fear or the convenience of not bearing the blame for failure to achieve happiness that precipitates people to blindly follow others, or worse yet, to give up on life totally.

Where then should you look?

How wonderful it would be if we entered life with a script, a blueprint, along with a vigilant mentor who would present us with truth to display the beauty contained in a mind at peace.

How comforting to share our lives from birth to death with an omnipresent guide, a guardian to keep us on the true path of our potentiality.

Where would we find our guide?

If you were your own child, what would you tell yourself about your current actions and attitude?

Engaged in a conversation of life, what advice would you give yourself?

If I was the mentor to my own questions, how would I answer them?

EC

THE PARADOX

Thank God for the evils that are of this world, for a soul weighed down by strife, not broken, rebounds to heights unattainable to that of the coddled spirit.

CONTENTS

I	The Darkness	8
II	The Dawn	9
III	The Awakening	13
IV	The Rains	22
V	The Reflection	27
VI	The Challenge	32
VII	The Growth	38
VIII	The Reawakening	43
IX	The Race	50
X	The Garden	55
XI	The Development	59
XII	The Truth	65
XIII	The Twilight	68
XIV	The Dusk	70
XV	The Darkness	79
XVI	The Beginning	81

12:01 **The Darkness**

THE PLENISHING* WOMB OF DARKNESS AND
COMFORT IS LEFT BEHIND   MY ADVENTURE
BEGINS

Why do I fear the darkness?

"Do not feel despondent, a child must be left alone in
the dark to reach the next level of maturity.

When left in the dark do not cry, FEEL.

Though you cannot see outside in the dark, inward you
can see as clearly as if in sunlight at noon; for the
cessation of external stimulus is necessary for you to
develop trust in your feelings.

Occasionally you must enter a fog to see the strongest
light. Be not afraid of the dark for there you will find
yourself, there you will find your life."

* PLENISHING - the initial source of nurture

The Dawn

THE MORNING IS THE CHILD OF THE DAY
MY EYES OPEN FOR THE FIRST TIME AND I FEEL THE
LIGHT CLEAR THROUGH TO MY MIND

Why is the newborn so beautiful?

"Is a flower blessed with beauty for itself or for the pleasure of others?"

Where am I?

"It matters not where you are but who you are, for who you are is where you are."

Are there problems here?

"Yes."

Then this is hell.

"In hell there are no problems subsequently there is no growth.

In heaven there are problems which we continually grow from.

In earth there are problems we hope to grow from; therefore earth can be heaven or hell; for you are your own creator."

Creator? Am I not the creation?

"You are the creation that creates."

How can I create beauty?

"By being beautiful."

How can I create truth?

"By being truthful."

I want to know how to create a better life for myself.

"To create a better life you must be a better creation."

Can't you tell me how to just do it?

"You do not just do it; you must just be it."

But I am so weak.

"In your weakness lies your strength."

How can there be strength in weakness?

"There is strength in the knowledge of your weakness.

Does not the weakness of the frail infant inspire more loyal service than the commands of a president? Will not the hunger cries of a babe take precedent over the demands of all else?

The infant can only receive yet does not the baby's smile return to our hearts an exalted purity of joy unmatched by the grandest of earthly gifts? Therefore is not the weakness of an infant a powerful demonstration of strength? Admonish your self-pity; for does not the weakness of the baby dictate the strength of the parents?"

Isn't the strength of the parent greater than that of the infant?

"Is not the parent subservient to the whim of the babe?"

Well yes; then the helpless infant possesses the greater strength.

"Will not the helpless infant perish if not cared for?"

Then neither's strength is greater.

"Both are greater."

But isn't it true that the parent must now unselfishly give while the infant can only selfishly take? Isn't it greater to live for others than for ourselves?

"The baby lives for itself, yet does it not give the greatest richness of joy to others? We must live for ourselves and not for others; and nothing do we do more for ourselves than when we do for others. You do not give to others for others; you give to others for yourself."

Will I be rewarded if I remember to do for others?

"The act of giving carries its own reward. When you do a selfish act of selflessness forget it, for if you remember it, the remembrance is your reward. If you talk about it then your voice has been your due."

How do I continue as the infant to bring such intense happiness to others without even trying?

"The infant illuminates for it does not try, it simply is."

So all I have to do is live?

"Not just live. Let your joyous expression of living be so rich that it causes others to sing."

The Awakening

I am starting to play games now.

"It is good to play games but do not let the games play
you."

How can a game play me?

"When you forget the true objective of playing."

Which is?

"Which is the living interaction between participants.
There lies winning. The game is merely a forum, an
avenue through which you are tested. Win at all
expenses and what you have is an expensive loss."

But the world loves a winner.

"True, but in which world do you want to be recognized
as a winner?"

What do you mean which world?

"Set behind every pair of eyes is an observer of and
from a unique world."

Observing me?

"Observing your games."

What are these games in my life?

"Understanding that these games in life are the life in the games. The games, the tests, the adventures differ but the rules are constant."

What are the rules?

"The rules are not to kill yourself for death. Living things are important not dead creations. Do not live for dead things but rather live for the living rewards."

What are the living rewards?

"It is the Loving nature of relationships which give us wealth, for these remain in our soul as nourishment; materials and money after the initial elevation leave one still hungry, for in itself, bring naught to the true us. It is the feeling of love represented by these symbols, not the love of the awards themselves, which constitute living rewards."

The nature of what relationships?

"The purity of your relationship with your loved ones, your loved one and your Love."

Then what is the point of playing?

"See a child run. The child is happy just running though they run for no reason other than to run. Is the child happy because they are running or running because they are happy?"

Then should I be happy just playing and not strive?

"We are wanted to strive, to play, to struggle and to accomplish. We are pleasing when we exert ourselves for accolades of our own creation if, and only if, they are the result of following the Eternal directions."

So as long as I don't break the law?

"Moral or mortal law?"

What's the difference?

"The mortal laws can be whimsical creations which we serve instead of serving us. The Moral law cannot be broken for that will break us."

How would I be broken?

"If the accolades are sought as they often are, without the presence to comprehend that they represent temporal rewards for spiritual congruency, they then become polarized to suck out the life we sacrificed for them."

How can I strive for material wealth in this world without having my life sucked out by the very things I strive for?

"If creation is accomplished, with good beneficial results, from productive acts of service; then we are richly rewarded for passing obstacles which are strewn before us as enticements."

Is this that devil devising these obstacles, trying to keep me from God?

"Are not these temptations so you can find God?"

How can I avoid these allurements?

"Deviate not from your dreams! Strive onward, ignore the psuedosweet smell of deviation and when you reflect on the dire straits you almost chose you will see you avoided the stench which you rationalized to be sweet for expediency."

Then I will be great like those I have heard about!

"Guard against arrogance. Do not sing your own praises, for the echo of your words is its own pleasure and ends all future reward."

Has the Moral law been around since creation?

"Is creation a one time act or is it an ever living process?"

I don't know.

"No you mean you do not wish to think, for to think you must feel. Think with your mind to feel in your heart. Feel in your heart to unclog your soul. Unclog the arteries of your soul and behold the boundaries of your power."

What power can I have, I am only a child?

"The unborn sees heaven, the teen must traverse hell; a child sees God and adults see the stage."

I see God?

"You cannot not see God."

Where is God?

"Perhaps God is the I in you?"

How could God be in I; I is me, isn't it?

"Observe how language separates us from ourselves. See how we can be split into the subjective I, and the objective, me. One is cause, the other effect. One acts, the other acted upon. Me is encompassed and mastered within I.

I AM, is Divine; to me is mortal. Could it be that within this animal resides Divinity? Could it be that I is the Creator, or at least of the Creator; and me is the creation of Life?"

What is the easiest way to make it through life?

"Die early."

What?

"Close your heart and mind, numb your senses, stop trying, deny the expression of your being and you are dead."

I want to live a life doing good.

"What are good deeds?"

Those done in the name of God.

"The guise of God is used more in reprehensible acts of hate than in glorious deeds of good. For more people have died in the name of God than in that of the most vile tyrant."

How do we express love of God if not through a name?

"The ludicrousness of our nature is the sad fact that we think we can package God up and sell it. This can be likened to selling firewood advertised as a living tree.

Do not mistake the timber for the tree. Do not love the dead God, love the Living by living the Love. For is love proven by the empty utterance of words or through the pureness of truthful living?"

How will I know truth?

"Truth will know you."

How will truth know me?

"Look to your heart, sense your true self, feel what brings you joy. Then direct your senses to recover that which was lost to you when entering this world."

Will truth then find me?

"The virtues will come if the accommodations look inviting."

How can I make myself more inviting for the acceptance of truth?

"Be beautiful."

How?

"Appreciate beauty outside of yourself."

So have an appreciative pair of eyes.

"Turn you critical eye inward and your appreciative eye outward."

If I must do this shouldn't other children also do this?

"Should you not demand more of yourself and less of others?"

But shouldn't I love myself?

"Love not yourself, love the self within yourself."

I am important though aren't I?

"You only become important when you realize you are not important."

When I grow up will I know better?

"The stream of life carries your body but the soul sits on a lake. Physical growth is automatic; spiritual growth is work."

Working to learn?

"Working to unlearn your unlearnings."

Can adults help me?

"The child is the reflection of the adult; for the child to change the adult must change."

Is the parent responsible for the child?

"Who is responsible for the reflection; the creator of the image or the creator of the mirror?"

I wish I could grow up quicker.

"Children rush into adulthood so they can act like children; for the children want to be adults and adults strive to be like children."

Which is better?

"There is no better there just is."

The Rains

THE DAY GROWS HOTTER IT RAINS BUT I DO
NOT SEE NOURISHMENT I ONLY FEEL DAMPNESS

I am often afraid.

"That which you fear controls you. Therefore fear not
evil, fear only Good and let Good control you."

How should I fear good?

"Let your fear of Good embrace you forever to It. Fear
Good in the reaction to your action. Understand every
thought, every feeling, every act contains a seed of
repercussion; dread the force of the inevitable backlash
of not being Good."

Is good the opposite of evil?

"The opposite of evil is live. That which causes you
not to live is evil. Cast out the demons which
impoverish your life; for you are the creator of all your
demons."

Is not the devil the creator of demons?

"Is not God the creator of the devil?"

This all makes me nervous.

"That which makes us nervous is what gives spirit to life."

Is this spirit important?

"The only thing that separates us from dust is spirit."

Must growing up hurt?

"All growth and progress are accompanied by pain. Therefore if we let our fear of pain paralyze us, we will not grow. When we stop growing we soon ripen and die!"

Can I minimize the pain?

"Do not shy away from pain for this heat is the life that forges the crass metal into a sheathable* sword. It is the bitter experiences of our visitations which contain the sweet nectar of our days.

Understand this; it is only within the strength developed from the pain of the thorns that you will reach the beauty in the frailty of the rose."

Can I escape the pains of growth without scars?

"The etchings upon the heart are the inscriptions which bestow its worth."

This is useless I don't need to know this.

* SHEATHABLE - functional; useful

"Do not confuse ignorance with knowledge. Do not grow up thinking you know everything, for you will grow up learning that you have learned nothing."

You must give me the answers.

"You must first learn to appreciate education then you are ready to proceed with the education."

But if I ask I should receive!

"To receive a greater allowance you must undertake greater chores. You must make yourself worthy to receive and then ask yourself what you want."

Ask myself? Ask myself what?

"Just to know what your heart wants. Request, Repose, React and you shall have it; but never by the means you imagine!"

I feel like everyone is trying to control me.

"The individual who allows themself to be controlled by themself is powerful."

You don't understand, I must fit in.

"Do not try to fit in; try to rise above."

Then I should try to be different?

"Do not be different; be better."

Better than others?

"Better than the yourself that you were yesterday."

How can I improve when I am surrounded by dense people and those who don't listen to me?

"That which you negatively feel toward others is the reflection of your current weakness, and who is responsible for the reflection; the creator of the image or the creator of the mirror?"

How should I deal with people?

"Understand each person is an individual experience."

And experience is the greatest teacher...right?

"If experience is the greatest teacher then mistakes are your homework."

By all means can you tell me just one of my mistakes?

"Placing your perceived friends above your perceived enemies."

Why is that such a mistake?

"You should trust your enemies. Often enemies are better friends."

How can that be?

"Your friend can hurt you more deeply than any enemy, for an enemy cannot betray you and betrayal is the most painful infliction one can plunge into the heart of a friend while purging their own quintessence."

Why is betrayal so painful?

"It is the curse from the lips which have kissed you which burns deepest, and those who love you most dearest are most apt to betray you."

Maybe it's better not to have friends.

"True friendship is a rare and precious jewel, a magnificent richness to share. Just be leery of false jewels that are actually burdensome rocks. Let the chains concealed in the name of friendship enslave yourself to the views of no one and no one group."

Great, how do I keep all this from happening?

"Keep pure your relationships with your loved ones, yourself and Life."

The Reflection

THE LIGHT PIERCES THROUGH THE CLOUDS TO DISPLAY THE GRANDEUR OF LIFE BROUGHT ON BY THE OPPRESSION OF THE RAINS

What should I do during the dark times?

"Just be."

Stop telling me useless stuff. Be what?

"Be a star!"

What do you mean...a musical star, a theatrical star, a star athlete..what?

"Be a personal star; the professional stardom can follow. But the luminescence of the person will shine deeper and longer than the one-dimensional brightness of the professional star. During dark times the true star gives the strength of light."

How can I become a personal star?

"Turn your light inward to work on your personal character."

If I want to shine outward like a star shouldn't I work on the outside, not my insides?

"It is the inner energy which illuminates. Like a star be bright, warm and attractive by being a giver of light; for you will attract good by emitting good."

Do I do this by living a life of love?

"You do this by loving Life!"

My own life?

"All Life. If you do not love Life, Life will not love you."

How do I show life I love it?

"Love of Life is shown in accomplishments that benefit others. Invest in Life, invest in relationships, work on the living and bury the dead!"

Then I should tell the people in my life I love them.

"Speak not of love; Feel it."

What if I don't love someone?

"Do not judge, just feel."

I have the right to speak my mind!

"Must you judge everything, everyone, everytime? You do not see the world behind another's eyes; therefore you can never judge them through yours! You can only share your feelings as you attempt to understand."

That seems pretty difficult.

"It is the easiest thing to do and it is the hardest."

I am afraid to love.

"Love is inborn; fear is learned."

You're wrong, for if I don't love I can't be hurt.

"If you truly love you cannot be injured. For if you love someone for themself and not for yourself you create a vulnerability which is invulnerable."

What if I love someone and the love is not returned?

"You love for your own sake, if your love is dependent on reciprocation then you do not yet know pure love for that is lust."

What is the difference between love and lust?

"Love is your creation from within; lust is created by another from without. Love is feeling; lust is possession. Lust and you are controlled as a slave to the person or thing which creates you; love and you are in control, for your feelings are truly yours, independent of the feelings or actions of another."

How will I know which is which?

"Time reveals all truths. True love flourishes with time; lust dissipates."

What about the loss of a loved one?

"The loss of a loved one perpetuates the gain of one love. For the same spirit of love which created you, came out to be visible and has returned to you in its purest form. The we has become I. So continue to love, for they are within you always."

OK, so I love others, whether they love me or not, but this loving my enemies stuff is nonsense. How can I love people who are mean or make me mad?

"No one makes you mad for it is your choice to become angry. Love those who you choose to become angry at, for they reveal yourself to yourself. It is they who add substance to your existence."

What about those who criticize me?

"Praise is a tasty dessert when justly deserved; fulfilling but unnecessary, for you know your own strengths. Rightful criticism is essential food for growth and scornful denunciations sustain your stature by silent abstinence."

Why should I be nice to those who oppose me?

"Anyone can take down an obstructing tree with an axe. It takes a person of vision to plant a seed."

What does all this perennial loving exactly accomplish for me?

"Choosing to act with love instead of reacting with hatred allows you to remain your own creator instead of someone else's creation; for that which you hate will always be your master."

But hate is very strong.

"Hate is the strongest indication of weakness! Love is the powerful symbol of unshakable strength!"

How can I best display this great strength?

"FORGIVE"

Ouch.

The Challenge

I CONTINUE TO LIVE AND LEARN   EARLIER CRISES
NOW ARE INTERESTING STORIES   LIVING REVEALS
THAT LIFE DOES NOT REVOLVE AROUND ME
RATHER I REVOLVE AROUND LIFE   ENVELOPED
IN THE SUN OF LIFE I CAN BASK IN IT   BURN IN
IT   OR BE BLIND TO IT

I keep learning but most of the time I don't seem any smarter.

"True knowledge humbles; falsehood exalts."

Then I should be humble, no matter how great I become.

"Do away with false pride. Do not think you are superior, for greater knowledge should humble you not exalt."

If I have a great idea why shouldn't I brag?

"Think not things come from us, for as a laden sponge is compressed dry of its inner holdings; so too will it be with us."

How can I know things that are not from me?

"Knowledge is believing in what you know; faith is believing in what you do not know."

It is difficult to act solely on faith.

"Yes, there is security in denial. However, beliefs bring us the future; facts are security for staying behind in the past. Belief precedes discovery."

What should I believe?

"That which you know is true."

Where do I find the wisdom to know what is true?

"In your book."

What book?

"Everyone should write their own book to find all wisdom is contained in their own soul. Do not wait for wisdom to start your book, begin writing and the wisdom will come.

Write a book for your own reading, for your own knowledge, for your own direction. Write your childhood dreams into a theatrical production for you to live out.

Write your own testament tying yourself to God. You write it, read it, live it and love it.

How Great Is Your Novel With No Ending."

My book? I can't write a book. I have no time for such an undertaking!

"NO TIME! You are truly blind to your own soul, for you see the clock yet neglect the moments. All you have...is TIME! Your time is your life. If you have no time for this critical time of sustaining insight, you have no life."

I want my life to mean something. How can I change the world if I'm at home writing my own book?

"Your outer world is a reflection of your inner world; for that which is inside is outside. Make yourself truthful and beautiful and your world will reflect truth and beauty."

How can I create outside beauty from the inside? I have no such skills and the world does not give me anything beautiful to work with!

"Admonish your self-pity. Does not the lowly oyster convert the irritating grain of sand into a precious pearl? It is given the most insignificant of earthly materials yet does it not create external beauty from its internal workings? Are you not given more both externally and internally than the mollusk?"

But there are so many things wrong with this world.

"There are many things wrong with your perception of your world, for the world is perfect whether we like it or not."

How can the world be perfect with so much misery?

"Its perfection lies in its imperfections. Suffering uncovers greatness; hunger inspires growth; tragedy reveals humanity; death brings life anew."

How could God let such horrible tragedies happen?

"Tragedies create goodness. The tragedies of life serve as the fertile grounds for the birth of heroes. The heroes then serve as models to inspire others."

How can I inspire when no one is observing me?

"The actor or actress cannot see the audience but knows they are being watched in their performance. So too should you perform as the hero in your dreams for you have an Eternal Audience and Director, and your performance will be known."

Why are there so many bad people?

"Good people sometimes do bad things."

Why can't we have world peace?

"At this point in our development we are not yet ready. If we had world peace today, tomorrow we would end up killing each other."

When should I fight for my rights?

"The only one who benefits from a fight are the spectators. Be careful; for you give life to that which you fight, as its strength will rise to match your aggression. You will add substance to your perceived opponents."

Then what should I do?

"BE PURE; and you can never be broken."
"BE BEAUTIFUL; and you have won the unwinnable fight."
"BE RIGHTEOUS; and you shall have victory even in death."

What if "they" wrong me?

"There is no 'they' there is only you and I, us and we."

Can the evils of this world be ridden?

"The evils of the world are here, for without them what would give our lives meaning? What would prompt minds to engage in deep progressive thought? What would motivate our hearts to display love, mercy and kindness? What would spark the soul to search for truth, and bring us to the threshold of its eternal source? What would be the impetus for God to become manifest in magnificent acts of purity?

When we make dispensable these currently indispensable REASONS for pure thoughts, feelings and acts; these REASONS will cease to exist!

Think, Feel, Do of greatness, of purity, of truth... and you will extinguish evil."

The Growth

THE AWKWARD TIME OF QUESTIONS CONTINUE
INTO THE QUESTIONING TIME OF AWKWARDNESS

How do I find who I am?

"Lose your conception of who you are."

Why do some people have less challenges than me?

"No one coasts through life. We are all tested according to our own abilities. Understand this: there are no 'lucky' ones. Individuals with seemingly greater attributes also·have imprinted from their souls greater expectations."

How do I find acceptance?

"If you seek acceptance from without you are dooming yourself to mediocrity. Seek acceptance from within for you can truly belong to none but yourself."

I want to get others to notice me.

"Then get others to notice themselves."

What do I need to do to accomplish great things?

"If you want to accomplish great things in your life, spend more time doing nothing. This means absolutely nothing. Forego the temptation to partake in time absorbing diversions.

The moments between the seconds are yours, and the Bread which sustains your faith will rise up to fulfill the opening of these hours which only you can create.

It is in these restive states of nothingness, as the shadows succumb to the soul, that you will find everything."

What is everything?

"960 hours of nothingness and you will know."

I don't understand.

"Understand you are not yet developed enough to understand."

How do I go about becoming successful or happy?

"You do not become successful or happy, you simply are or you are not."

But what if I'm not?

"Just be."

Here we go again. I don't get it.

"Few ever do."

Try me.

"There are those who are successful in all different fields of endeavor who were a success before they even started. They just were. It does not matter what techniques these people used to reach their goals for each individual was successful in being successful primarily; then success became manifested in the contributions of their work secondarily."

So I work on myself first then I work on making 'alot' of money, right?

"In societies the most inert and useless items are converted into a medium of material exchange: stones and rocks, minerals and metals, shells and feathers, bones and paper. Though lifeless and abundant, these are hoarded and worshiped above the unique beauty of your own living wealth. Instead of working to be a collector, work at being a collectable."

But I want to have lots of money.

"You mean you want to earn lots of money."

What's the difference? As long as I've got it.

"An excess of materialism is an enervating burden; receive with joy retribution equal to or less than your contribution. Deny excess for it is a golden anchor."

What if I get lucky and win wealth?

"Do not confuse money with wealth. When you work for what you have, all you have is yours. If you want to destroy someone, give them money or credit which they did not earn nor deserve."

How about you give me the money first and then I'll become worthy of it?

"If you are not ready for responsibility; you are not ready for success."

Why do I have to work on my person so much if I just want to be a financial success?

"The more of a person you are, the more money and success you deserve, and the less you need."

But when I am rich I can do great things.

"What great feat was ever performed while living in luxury? Great things are done when one is striving to become truly rich."

But I know my life will be better if I could become rich or famous.

"Do not long for fame or money; for neither have ever brought happiness to a troubled soul. Long for nothing and you shall have everything."

What things should I ask for, to be happy?

"Ask not for things, ask for feelings. For if we need things to evoke feelings we become slaves to our servants, for naught can bring us these feelings but ourselves."

Then how do I find perfect happiness?

"The way to achieve perfect happiness is to never strive for it. You are the happiest you will ever be at this moment, so be the happiest that you can be."

What about future happiness?

"The future never comes, for it is already here."

That is stupid.

"Guard well what you say, for words are alive. Words are investments which can be secure or risky, profitable or detrimental. Of the utmost importance, they must be true."

Why is life so difficult?

"Life is simple we make it difficult."

The Reawakening

WHAT TIME IS IT : IT IS TIME

What if my life doesn't seem right?

"Then you need to either work on your singing or change your song."

My singing? My song? What song?

"YOU! You are the song and the singer."

Riddles, always riddles, why can't I ever receive a straightforward answer? Why is every answer a paradox? How can I be the song and the singer?

"You are the song, you are the singer, you are the paradox.

LIFE IS A PARADOX-an illustrious continuum of notes construing a melody that seem random at the time but in repose devise a definite, divine, drama to which we both appear in and observe."

That's an amazing revelation!

"Today's revelations are tomorrow's cliches."

How does this song that sings idea help me with my messed up life?

"By understanding we can easily live our life out of alignment. Just as a singer who sings out of tune; a pleasurable melody is disrupted and misperformed*. We must clear our obstructions to hear how the melody should be. Listen as you sing, when you are out of tune set yourself back in line and the melody will be sweet, not just to others but to yourself and your Divine Audience.

To know if you are off key you must reflect quietly and listen, lest you continue down the scale which is not yours and your song is a forced, haphazard conglomeration, offensive to your vibratory spirit.

Take this daily time, listen to the recording you are creating, if it feels good sing it more vociferously. If it is not sweet then it is not your song. Either you picked the specific verse for the wrong reasons or it was chosen erroneously for you. Choose your song within the scale of your strength, with the words you love.

No two performers entertain in the same exact way but the basic rules are constant. The rules are the eternal purities to which our lives are anchored to. The foundation to build upon as we evoke our personal joys when we uniquely perform our song, chosen by us and for us, according to our given Talents.

* MISPERFORMED - improper utilization of skills

So sing your song, there are all to choose from; continue selecting until you uncover the one which elates your soul. Choose it, Sing it, Listen to it with truthful ears not biased ones. Improve it if it does not sound right. Change it if it does not feel right. If it sounds right and feels right sing it louder and share this joy with others for that is the seeding which culminates in the reason for song."

Don't I sing for myself?

"All self-serving acts are self-defeating. The most selfish thing we can do is to be selfless. Practice singing for yourself, sing your masterpiece for others."

No one ever told me I have to practice my song, I thought I just sing.

"Then how could it be anything but atrocious? You must review your song, you must practice singing; you must review your life, you must practice living. You must work to relax, to let life flow from your lips so effortlessly that none realizes the fantastic effort involved in creating the performer they see in front of them."

How do I choose the right work or profession?

"First work on being a professional person, then be a person working on a profession."

How do I find a great job?

"Be a great worker."

What profession or job should I choose?

"That in which you can provide the greatest service to others."

How do I earn the most money that I can?

"The fewer people who can do your job your way, the greater your worth. The more difficult you are to replace the more money you righteously deserve. Only you decide how easily replaceable you are."

Should I alert others to my hard work?

"The more noise you make the less you will be heard; for the whisper gathers more listeners than the shout."

How does silently doing a good job do me any good?

"Your reputation will reach out to far more people than you yourself ever could."

How much time should I dedicate to work?

"You should constantly be engaged in constructive activities. Time is an elusive richness, present everywhere yet rarely utilized. Time must never be hung out, for time ignored can never be retrieved. Time must be embraced, never ignored."

I meant how much time should I focus on my job?

"Seldom do people look back and proclaim that more time should have been spent at their respective jobs. More commonly it is wished that to have to do over again, it would have been more fulfilling to have invested and cherished more time with loved ones and purposefully enjoying life."

Well, how hard should I work at my employment?

"Work as hard as you can, but for your own worth, not for money only. Money is paper, it is the perception that is valuable. Change your perception to value the living and instead of having false wealth, you will be truly wealthy. For your peace of mind is worth more than a piece of paper."

Then I should work less and play more.

"Play more at work and you will need not to work so hard to play."

What kind of wages can I receive for playing?

"Those who play for a living receive the highest wages."

How can I be successful playing for a living?

"By loving what you do and doing what you love."

But I hate my job! In fact I hate my life!

"Blame not your job nor your life for your decision to deviate from your dreams."

What profession is best?

"People are not judged on their respective profession but rather in the performance of their profession."

But don't I have to be ruthless to compete?

"Is not the bluebird fed while the vulture must scrounge? Be a bluebird and sing and you shall be fed. However be only on the prowl and you must hunt always, for it will never be given freely to you."

Why does it matter whether I get something by singing or hunting, just so long as I get it?

"If something is done for you grudgingly you still owe a price. If given to you gladly, then you have already paid it."

But I must take mine, certainly there is not enough riches to feed everyone's wishes.

"Again we are like birds scampering for the crumbs but nervously fearing the hand which feeds us. Thankfully accept the crumbs, fear not the hand and we shall sit at the table of Eternity. We fight over finite crumbs instead of joyfully singing for Eternal resources."

Yes but what about my life in this world?

"Be concerned less with my and more with I."

I would like to know how to live in this world.

"We are our own worlds. Independent in our inner struggles, interdependent in our existence. Help another with a clue that has helped yourself and you free your heart to receive."

Since I am independent, why do I care what happens to others? What effect is there on me?

"We are independent and interdependent like the organs in our body. Though individual in function, all need to work together for the body of society to properly operate. We need to take care of the entire aspect from brain to bowel. For even the lowly regarded bowel, if neglected, can choke the life out of our existence."

So I should help others at all cost?

"It is marvelous to love others as you love yourself; however what virtue is there in loving others to your detriment?"

The Race

THE SKY IS THE SAME BUT AN INVERTED IMAGE OF
ITS FORMER SELF   THERE IS MUCH DAYLIGHT
LEFT BUT I GROW CONCERNED THAT THE DAY
CONTROLS ME INSTEAD OF I THE DAY

What should I do for money and possessions?

"Let material wealth serve you; do not you serve it."

But I want to be respected.

"A person who depends on money to garnish them
with respect lives a paper existence. For it is not what
is inside the person that is respected, rather it is what
is inside the pocket and purse which is desired. A full
pocket or purse without knowledge of self weighs one
down; a full heart will always raise one up. How
fortunate are those said to be poor, thought to be ugly,
perceived to be handicapped, for they know their true
worth."

Then what should I do?

"Do what you would do if money did not exist and receive with joy all you are worthy of. Again do not sell your life for death. True wealth cannot be seen, it is felt. It is counted by the multitude of smiles from your heart and those you create upon the lips of others. Living senses can never be satiated by dead creations. Live for these living feelings."

How will I find these living feelings?

"It is as if there is a spring of Life and we are all as ponds. The more we open up ourselves, the greater will be our fill."

What enables me to receive this pool of life?

"The roots of the implanted tree are the means by which it receives nourishment for growth in this life."

What are my roots?

"Our roots are our senses, five we know, more we are not yet aware. The farther our roots reach out, the greater our intake of Eternal resources and true nourishment. The detriments of a closed mind, heart, and soul chokes off our roots and denies our limbs of richness and our lives of growth."

So tell me how can I expand my roots?

"See with your mind, hear with your mind, taste with your mind, smell with your mind, feel with your mind, sense with your mind; for your mind is the doorway to your heart which is the external passage to the soul. Know your soul and only then will you know the euphoria of your dreams."

What if I don't know my soul?

"You can make improvements or excuses, the choice is yours."

Can someone show me how?

"No one can do this enrichment for you. Obtain clues from others, follow the lessons of the Unbounded Soul but reserve for yourself the final decree. For mastery is inherent; subservience is fear."

Do I not follow the Unbounded Soul now?

"We are amused by the Unbounded Soul but we focus on capitalizing upon, instead of learning to become the Soul and letting the Soul become us."

How do I learn to become and let?

"By starting the journey, the life long journey which takes you everywhere while going back to whence you came."

How can this journey of life take me everywhere and leave me where I started?

"Life is cyclic; you must end where you began."

Then why live?

"The human race can be likened to a marathon race. One cannot decide to run such a race then just do it. No, you must be able, before you do ably. Perseverance, adherence to knowledge and true principles with a daily regiment of progressive living will enable you to do what was once inconceivable. You return after the race as you were, where you were before the race, yet you are different. That difference is why you live."

Where is this taught?

"In all interactions there must be a gain of knowledge. That which you are ready to learn will be revealed to you. The voice of a neighbor carries the wisdom of God, if you hear with ears that truly hear."

So I will be given teachers.

"Everyone you meet is your teacher. You must be ever vigilant to learn from every voice, every scene, every experience. Even if you learn how not to do something, you have still learned."

How can I become a teacher?

"By forever remaining a student. The greatest teacher is the student and the best way to learn is to teach."

Can I use artificial means to bring my mind to higher awareness?

"Thoughts, words and acts, spoken or performed, by one drugged, drunk or angry lead more to regrets than enlightenment."

The Garden

I AM WEARY OF LOOKING OUT AT THE SUN AND
TURN TO LOOK INTO MY OWN SHADOW WHICH
MOVES AS A PART OF ME AND YET HAS NO LIFE

We all cast the same shadows don't we?

"We all share the same fears, do we not?"

Are we all the same?

"Yes."

Are we all different?

"Yes."

How can we all be different and yet be the same?

"We are all given our own life in this garden by the
same Gardener."

And do we represent different species?

"If a tree bears apples it can be confined to being called
an apple tree. If a tree bears oranges it can rightfully
be labeled as an orange tree, for it is predictable and
limited in its produce. What would you call a tree which
was unpredictable in its produce?"

I guess it would be called a produce tree.

"Then do not confine yourself or others to labels."

Is it true that the Gardener has special preferences among those in the garden?

"God Has No Favorites!"

But I've been told about certain groups of people, that they are dangerous.

"Far more dangerous is the attempt to use fear to alienate you from your neighbor, and to categorize precious embodiments of the living God into convenient packages."

Then how should I best judge others?

"If you still feel you must categorize people; the best way to judge your feelings towards a particular race, religion, gender or group is through one person at a time."

Tell me, how do I keep from categorizing individuals into groups?

"Base your feelings on another's character, not color; on their soul not sex; on how their time is spent not where their money is sent."

If we are all the same, from the same God, why do we have so many different religions?

"We attempt to slice up and serve that which must be taken as a whole."

How does this happen?

"We, the creation, create a creator who is in fact our creation. We then proceed to serve our creation instead of our Creator."

How can I best serve our true Creator?

"Our true Creator is Love and true creation is an act of Love. Therefore love Life's creations, as the Life Creator."

Is there a religion which is best?

"It is not the label of a group which makes it good, it is the people within. It is not the techniques which matters, only the validation within your heart which does.

Labels and techniques of themselves are inert, it is the direction of their use which brings us closer or farther from the light. Use the techniques to worship; do not worship the techniques."

Which groups are best for me?

"The primary function of a group or organization is to benefit itself, as it must for survival. As long as the group's thoughts and actions are congruent with your own, engage with a pure conscience. For the organization must serve you as it benefits itself, else you are serving it. And you must never become a servant to an it; an it must always serve you."

What if I don't agree with the group I am in?

"If the group's thoughts are not yours do not blindly follow; for in that instance you cease to exist."

The Development

THOUGH I AM SURROUNDED BY MANY I REALIZE I
AM ALONE   THOUGH TO NEVER FEEL LONELY I
TRY TO UNDERSTAND THAT THERE IS AN
ABUNDANCE OF LIFE WITHIN THAT IS GREATER
THAN THE SUM OF LIFE AROUND

Why do I not get that which I strongly desire and think I'm worthy of?

"That which you love more than Purity must be denied you or taken away. Love Living more than all and you shall be given all."

But why don't I get what I ask for?

"We are given the seed of that which we ask. If we were given the ripen fruit it could never be ours, for we must nurture the growth of our dreams for them to be ours."

Will I ever find a perfect relationship?

"Your relationships will be as perfect as you are."

How can the dreams of sweet loving relationships turn into such sour nightmares?

"Remember if a romance parts, do not cling to the person who in the past shared a feeling with you, for growth must occasionally sever bonds. That time is the past; savor the memory but live in the present.

If you mistakenly assume that you need another to feel love, never will you find such a person, for one does not exist. Your relationships will predictably pattern themselves to this underdevelopment in your character and you will remain a slave to pseudo-relationships until you learn your teachings."

What teachings?

"You are loved and you alone are responsible for the feeling of love, not another. Then and only then shall you be capable to partake in blissful relationships."

Sometimes I feel life is too hard, I am too weak and I should just end it.

"If you are contemplating suicide, wait until you are happy."

Are you ridiculing me?

"I wish to keep you from ridiculing yourself."

How can I escape my problems?

"Do not escape from yourself; conquer yourself."

How then should I deal with horrors?

"Your fiercest tragedies, your most horrific detriments, deserve the melodies of your most thunderous laughter."

People will think me crazy.

"The best way to stay sane is to be crazy."

How should I deal with anger?

"To conquer that which angers you, you must laugh at it. When someone wrongs you ... laugh. Amends will be made to you if you do not ask for, or expect it. Laugh at the judicious fallacy and frailty of the mortal justice system. Be assured the Moral system is ever present, never failing and subtly overpowering.

In laughter there is freedom. Laugh at those who malign, and do not malign those who laugh at you. Laugh at yourself and God is pleased. Take your responsibilities seriously but do not take yourself too seriously.

Laugh at the afflictions which befall you and the world will cradle you as a loving mother would come to her beautiful child."

Then laughter is good?

"Laugh at the afflictions of others and your vileness will rust the sparkle off your soul."

When then is laughter good?

"When used as a tool to confront your fears. When you turn your serpents into swords. For that which you detest or fear will continue to impede your development, until you challenge the fear directly and observe the possibility of its pain melt from the confrontation."

Can we not just run from our fears?

"That which we strive to avoid will circle and encircle us, until we stop running and gaze directly toward its fangs to see it is not a snarl but a smile."

How about just distancing ourselves from our fears?

"To avoid getting hurt from a punch, stand close to the fist at all times. Embrace that which frightens you and it cannot hurt you."

Will the work never end?

"Life's challenges can be likened to cleaning dishes. The moment the sink is clean, another meal results in more labor. The only way to stop the work is to stop the meals."

Will the struggles never end?

"To live is to struggle, for it is the struggles of your life which give you life. So enjoy the struggle and you will enjoy life."

Why should I enjoy my struggles?

"Do not choose to be miserable as you strive. For be assured you most certainly would be miserable when you are left nothing to strive for."

But my struggles are so hard.

"Those who struggle too hard can work themselves to death. Those with no struggle are already dead."

Why are my struggles accompanied by so much pain?

"Pain is often the strongest voice of God."

Telling me what?

"Apparent misfortunes are frequently no more than guardrails keeping us on the true road and impeding a far worse disaster. So curse not the collision for you were saved from a more catastrophic fate."

Is there a way to ease my pain?

"Ease another's pain. For if every person made an effort to help just one other; we would all have someone helping us through the day."

And will doing this in a day help my lifetime?

"**Your lifetime is a day.** So live today, enjoy today. Do not postpone your life one more day."

How do I prevent my life from being mundane?

"By you not being mundane. Dream .. then do. What you think is true .. is. The world is perception, a culmination of thoughts. Think right thoughts and the life will follow. Think shallow thoughts and life will be shallow. Think beauty, think truth, think deep richness in the engagement of life and this is so."

That's fine for an idealist, but I'm a realist.

"An idealist lives in the world of their own choosing; a realist lives in the world chosen by others."

Then that which I think about, is what will happen?

"That which you think cannot happen ... will. That which you fear will happen ... already has. That which you hope does or does not happen ... will unravel to display your development."

It will what?

"It will work out for the best."

The Truth

I SEE THE DAY STARTING TO FADE   THOUGH STILL
BEAUTIFUL NOW I WONDER MORE ABOUT WHY
WHY AM I DIFFERENT THAN THE ANIMALS

What is the worst evil?

"Lies."

Lies! Little old lies? Everything is worse than lies.

"Lies are the parents of the other evils. For lies are the
most acceptable form of wrongs and initiate the
progression away from truth."

What if others lie?

"Show them truth."

This sounds difficult.

"It is the easiest thing to do and that is what makes it
so difficult."

Where can the strength be found to do these things?

"In truth."

Why is truth so strong?

"Truth is light from the beacon of God; lies are our own erroneous creation - a mortal made fabrication of expediency which shrouds temporarily but burns in time."

Where can I find truth?

"In all things that are of themselves. In the paradoxes of life; there you will find truth."

What if we need to lie to avoid punishment?

"If you have to lie you are already punished."

What is the first step?

"Stop the lies! Spouse to spouse; government to people; parent to child; humanity to itself. Stop exploiting and start imploiting*. Stop the lying and the veil obstructing truth and beauty shall be lifted."

Wow, that sounds like we would be in heaven.

"We do not always dive into the pool, sometimes the pool comes to envelope us."

Are you suggesting that we may not have to go to a special place to be in heaven?

"Is not God everywhere? Does not God reside in heaven? Then could not heaven be everywhere?"

* IMPLOITING - engagement in words or activities which utilize others for their own benefit

With such glorious possibilities, why do we lie?

"To create false beauty."

How so?

"The skin may wrinkle and bleed yet it is a beautiful and perfect design; be it judged ugly or beautiful by temporal eyes. No number of layers of the most eloquent garment can hide the ulcerated skin of a treacherous wretch. To the outside eyes there is elegance and beauty, yet the truth is, on the inside there is grotesqueness which will erode through the silks. For time erodes all fabrications and reveals all truths."

What can be done about the damage to the beauty of the Divine creation which was attempting to be covered up by the lies of our mortal creation?

"Only the wretch can conjure the cure. For only atonement to others, to self and to Life remedies the wounds."

The Twilight

AS MY DAY STARTS TO DESCEND ASCENSION
OCCURS ON THE YOUNG ONES   THAT WHICH
WAS IMPORTANT AT NOON IS NOW SWEET IN
REMEMBRANCE   GROWING TO REALIZE THERE
ARE OTHERS FOR WHICH I AM RESPONSIBLE MY
RESPONSIBILITIES ARE BINDS OF JOY   TO ENJOY
AS A CHILD WHILE CARING FOR OTHERS I MUST
REMAIN CHILDLIKE AND NO LONGER CHILDISH

*How can I show my dear precious child how not to
make the same mistakes I did?*

"You cannot live your child's life for them. To gain
strength and knowledge they must journey alone. You
can only be a guidance not a vehicle."

*How do I help my child become the person I think they
should?*

"By you being the person you want your child to
become."

Why is parenting so demanding?

"That which offers the richest rewards must require
the greatest work. As you request from Life so must
you exude patience with those who demand from you,
for the answer you return to your child will be the
identical reply you yourself receive."

Can I discipline my child without hurting them?

"If you want to hurt your child, fail to discipline."

How should I discipline?

"Discipline your child as you wish to be kept true. As you give to your children so too will Life give to you. If you take, so too shall it be taken from you."

What if my child does not understand why I am doing what I must?

"The child cannot always understand the parent's discipline, neither can the adult always understand Divine reprimands. God reprimands us for our own benefit, for God needs nothing; so too should we reprimand for our child's benefit, never for ourselves."

How will I or my son or daughter know what we should do?

"Time is the great educator."

The Dusk

DUSK IS A REFRESHING TIME AS WELL AS AN
OMINOUS SIGN

Why was I here?

"You are exactly where you are and who you are for
reasons not for your knowing. But know this, you alone
are responsible for your performance regardless of
circumstances."

How can life's events seem so random?

"Being happy or unhappy, successful or unsuccessful
is a moment to moment occurrence; stop doing what
made you that way and you will no longer be."

Is nothing given freely?

"Our lives were given to us; all else we must work
for."

Do our spirits mature as our bodies do?

"Our bodies grow older automatically, we grow up only
through work."

What's the difference?

"Age and wisdom are not the same. One is gained through surviving the years, the other through experiencing them."

Will I stay young by acting young?

"Some of us try to recapture youth by doing things we never would have done when we were young."

Why is there change?

"To keep things constant."

Why can't things stay the same?

"Nature accepts change, as her leaves alter colors; and the loss of life, when there is the falling away of dead branches, with the serene equanimity of awareness that this is necessary to accept new gifts. For without change or loss there can be no gain."

I want to return to the past.

"We look fondly to the past and grimly to the future, yet today is the future's past. Why do we not look happily at it whilst we are performing in it. It is as when we honor people after they are gone instead of when they are with us. We remember only the good. Why not remember the good of today and people while both are in the present."

Why can't I get all this? I'm sorry for my ignorance.

"Do not apologize for being human. No one is perfect; we live to try as we try to live."

So if I commit a wrong, do I have to apologize?

"Do not just be sorry, be educated. Gain wisdom from a wrong and be prepared with a light heart for retribution, for it must be delivered. Curse the ensuing punishment and you are sentenced again."

Life seems futile.

"Then have fun with it."

Show me how I can have fun with futility.

"We can take pride in knowing that no matter what we do, the next generation will say we did it wrong."

How can we do it right?

"Be righteous."

Do we control ourselves or are we controlled?

"We can be likened to chess pieces, with different talents and abilities. We have the privilege of opting to bring ourselves up to our potential through ethics, study and hard work. We can build character internally and raise ourselves from pawns to kings or queens.

Where we are positioned in the grand scheme of our personal encounters is not in our control. The movements occur through Fate as dictated by the force of Nature which is controlled by God.

Our capability to handle situations is in our control; the strategy behind each situation is in the control of God."

Why is there death?

"So there can be furthering of life; for we must empty our arms of present attachments to be ready to receive greater gifts."

Are there any answers in life?

"There can only be questions. For can the answers be revealed during the test, or only upon its completion?"

Then what is life?

"Life is an accumulation of experiences, each one like a pearl on a necklace. At the twilight of one's life the more experiences garnished, the greater the sparkle in the setting rays."

How do I collect these pearls?

"By collecting memories as opposed to materials."

How do I collect pearls of memories?

"By giving often; not of yourself but of God. Be a conduit, a portal revealing God through your good and understanding you are simply a medium through which you relieve the world's suffering by showing others that 'God Loves You.'

When you give, you give of Life. When you take, you rob from your own soul and fill it with human frailties. You already have everything you need but you do not realize it.

We live as a dog without its master; lost, lonely and sad. Understand that your Master is with you and loves you and will care for you if, and only if, you love unconditionally."

Is there a purpose to life?

"Life is the purpose. It is a continual test, which like all true tests forces our further development so we can advance to the higher level. Each crisis, every obstacle, all hopeless and unfair situations are progressive steps toward heaven."

Is life a battlefield?

"This life is the playground of the angels. There is not an angel between us that would not relish the chance to perform in your struggles."

How should I perform to benefit from my life struggles?

"Work! Work feverishly, daily on your personal development. Work to be and you shall do.

Be worthy and you shall receive.

Be beautiful in heart, mind and soul and you will see beauty in the most appalling of scenes.

Be truthful and your strength is insurmountable.

Do not be numb to the extravagance of simplicity, for the most exquisite of garments start as but a single thread. Let the thread of your life be simple, truthful, and beautiful. Know this is joyful living."

I can't always be working, what should I do when resting?

"In empty moments, as the second hand progresses quietly, sing your love for Life. During dark times smile in your awareness that you are ALIVE."

Is this suppose to help me understand life?

"Life is not to be figured out, it is to be lived. For life is and always will be a paradox - a constant barrage of contradiction, of irony, of inconquerable* mystery; a living, breathing game to be delved into and played with all your zest, all your intensity, all your being.

Scrape away the trifles and worries of your own creations, ignore the discord of dead things and savor the melodies of the living creations; the pinnacle of which is your life.

Your life is to be lived and enjoyed. Your struggles bring reward, your losses bring gain. When you give, you get, and what greater joy nurtures your soul than an undisclosed righteous act? What joy life can be! What an indulgent game of rapture to live a righteous life."

Life as a game?

"Chess, soccer, basketball are all games, this we clearly recognize for we created them. The game we do not comprehend as such is our very existence for we did not devise it."

But a game?

"How can it be anything but? Life, the game, is such a part of us that we do not see it. The eye sees all except itself, it only sees its reflection but that is but an image and can be distorted."

---

* INCONQUERABLE - that which cannot be overcome by force but by understanding

Distorted, how?

"When we obey the false majesty of earthly mediums to believe externity* grants us the rules to pleasure."

Where should I look then?

"The guidelines are blueprinted into our very fiber. Feel, do not be told, lest it be your inner voice, for it is the sweet sound whispering that which you seek. Our conscience is the seed of Life. Obey and nourish the conscience through purity and righteous feeling and the seed flourishes into a Divine garden."

How do I win?

"We are judged not on our temporal victories but on our true victory over self, in how we play this game. Do not strive to impress others. Only you know, even if you do not know, that which brings you the most intense of heartfelt satisfaction. The principles are universal, the techniques are your own. Live as you know you should."

How do I live then, as I know I should?

---

* EXTERNITY - self-appointed earthly experts who aggrandize themselves, generally to prompt actions which benefit themselves

"Do not be afraid and you cannot be manipulated.
Do not hate and you will have no master.
Do not envy and you will be admired.

Only a life of truth and beauty can bring you peace of mind; and only you are strong enough to create such a life. Be truthful, be beautiful and you shall share your body with Divinity.

Work for a feeling, play for a feeling, live for a feeling... the feeling of the heightened sublime enrichment of ecstasy which living, no, playing this game of living, in accordance with truth and beauty fulfills the Word of your Soul. This is how you live each day instead of dying each day."

The word of my soul? What word is that?

"The Word you wish used to describe who you are; for as you are remembered thus do you become."

Will I be remembered?

"Let your joyous expression of living be so rich that it causes others to sing and yes, you will be remembered."

Why do you repeat yourself?

"Why does time repeat itself in a day?"

I don't know.

"You will."

The Darkness

EVEN DARKNESS IS GROWTH   THE DAY GROWS
DARK

Why do we kill the most innocent of beings?

"Who lives longer, the sacrificial lamb or the murdering
wolf? Does not the lamb live in us; while the wolf
dies at death?

Strength can be gained in death. The greatest way to
perpetuate a person's beliefs is to kill the person. The
unsurpassed method to eternalize an idea is to separate
that spirit from it's mortal encasement. Kill the flesh,
free the soul.

A murderer slays not the victim but the self, for it is
not the blade which kills, it is the grip."

Is this the end?

"There are no endings only commencements."

How is that possible?

"Is not your sunset at the same time a sunrise
elsewhere?"

Then there are no endings.

"If there are only beginnings, what does that teach you?"

There are no absolutes.

"Including that one."

This stuff all sounds familiar.

"These thoughts are yours. These truths are recognizable, the words are quite old. Perhaps the words of these truths will rebecome your thoughts."

I certainly have learned much.

"You certainly have unlearned much, and what has your unlearning taught you?"

That life is a paradox - an illustrious continuum of notes construing a melody which appears random at the time but in repose devise a definite, divine, drama to which we both appear in and observe.

"Most importantly..."

Yes, which is most important?

"Remember You Are Loved."

11:59 THE DAY COMMENCES AND THE LIFETIME BEGINS

The Beginning

ORDER FORM

If you are unable to locate a copy of THE PARADOX in your local bookstore, please call **1 (800) 351-5450** for ordering information, or send a check or money order with this order form to: **Alexandria Publishing, 163 3rd Ave., Box 139, N.Y., N.Y. 10003.**

Ordered by

Name: _____
Address: _____
City, State, Zip: _____
Phone (in case order information is needed: ( ) _____

Ship to Address (if different from Ordered by Address)

Name: _____
Address: _____
City, State, Zip: _____

Method of Payment: ☐ Check   ☐ Money Order
Please make your payment **payable to: Alexandria Publishing**

Price Category	Price/copy	x	Qty.	=	Price
☐ 1 - 5	9.95				
☐ 6 - 10	8.95				
☐ 11 - 20	7.95				
☐ 21 +	6.95				

	Merchandise Subtotal $	
	Sales Tax	
	(N.Y. Residents add 8.25% sales tax)	
	Shipping and Handling	**FREE**
	TOTAL AMOUNT	

Thank You For Your Order!